CONTENTS

INTRODUCTION
CHAPTER ONE
STUDY ALL ABOUT BEES
Honey Bees Are Critical to the World's Economy
A Solid Climate Needs Honey Bees
Honey Bee Amicable Spaces Are Useful For Us As Well
Honey Bees Are Artistic Symbols
Various Honey Bees Have Various Characters
Imperiled Honey Bee Species
What Are The Reasons For Honey Bee Decay?
Without Honey Bees, We're In A Tough Situation
Honey bees and pesticides
Interface With Nearby Beekeeping Associations
CHAPTER TWO
BEEHIVE
How to Set Up Your Beehive
Find out About Beekeeping Assignments
CHAPTER THREE
BEEKEEPING SUPPLIES
Assemble Your Beekeeping Supplies
How to Gather Your Beekeeping Supplies
CHAPTER FOUR
BEEKEEPING HIVE SYSTEM
Ten-Frame Langstroth Hive
Eight-Frame Langstroth Hive
Top-Bar Hive
Warré Hive
How to Choose The Right Hive System
Some History
What's a Bee Looking For in a Home?
Hive Maintainance
The Inspection Process
Eliminate the Outer Cover
Eliminate the Inner Cover
Eliminate the Honey Super
Smoke the Second Deep Box
Check for Larvae
Search for Eggs
Supplant the Frames
Supplant the Second Deep and Honey Super
Supplanting the subsequent profound
Supplant the outer cover

CHAPTER FIVE
ORDER YOUR HONEY BEES
    How to Order Your Honey Bees
    Long Lane Honey Bee Farms
    B and B Honey Farm
    Sweet Mountain Honey
    How to Maintain Queenright Colony
CHAPTER SIX
INTRODUCE BEES TO THE HIVE
    How to Introduce Bees to the Hive
    What do I need to begin?
    Parts of a Package
    Introducing the Queen
    How to Keep Your Bees Healthy and Happy
    How to Control Overcrowding
    Outer signs that bees are likely to swarm
    Honey bees returning exhausted from the field
    Signs of overcrowding
    Reviewing inside a strong colony in spring
    Reviewing the brood box
    Noticing a dummy queen cell (also known as a play cup)
    Arising of a newly born worker bee
    Presence of drones in August (not long before springtime)
CHAPTER SEVEN
INSPECT YOUR BEEHIVE
    The Inspection Process
    Planning
CHAPTER EIGHT
BEEKEEPING TASKS BY THE SEASON
    Spring Tasks
    Summer Tasks
    Autumn Tasks
    Winter Tasks
CHAPTER NINE
HONEY BEES FEEDING
    When Do You Feed Bees?
    Instructions to Feed Bees
    Dust Patties Feeding
    Fondant and Sugar Candy Feeding
CHAPTER TEN
HARVESTING
    How to Open the Hive
    Eliminate the Outer Cover
    Eliminate the Inner Cover
    Eliminate the Honey Super
    Smoke the Second Deep Box
    Eliminate the Second Deep Box
    Eliminate the First Frame
    How to Remove Bees from the Hive
    Check for Larvae

Search for Eggs
Supplant the Frames
Supplant the Second Deep and Honey Super
Supplant the Inner Cover
How to Uncap the Honey
How to Extract the Honey
How to Filter & Bottle Your Honey
How to aim for Honey Quality Over Quantity
CHAPTER ELEVEN
HOW TO COMBINE HIVES
When to Combine Two Hives
The most effective method to Combine Hives
CHAPTER TWELVE
PROTECT BEES AND BEEHIVES FROM BEARS
How to Protect and Prevent Beehive From Bears
Beehive Proper Placement
Beehive Fencing
CONCLUSION

INTRODUCTION

If you are attracted to the possibility of keeping your bees, read on. I'll describe the fundamentals of beekeeping for newcomers, whether you're a backyard beekeeper, a hobbyist farmer, or a small farmer hoping to launch a business making honey and other bee supplies. It's pretty easy to learn how to grow bees. There are several aspects to consider before undertaking a beekeeping journey, so before sailing, first, evaluate if beekeeping is appropriate for you.

CHAPTER ONE

STUDY ALL ABOUT BEES

There are indeed a lot of beekeeping publications, and finding what you can about these adorable tiny creatures can help you get your hives off on the right way. Learn as far as you can so when your bees arrive, you'll be able to manage to keep your bees.

For What Reason Does the World Need Honey Bees?

Honey bees are crucial for a sound climate and solid economy. We depend on them and different creepy crawlies to fertilize most of our leafy foods. Be that as it may, honey bees are in danger and without them so is the world's food and economy. You can make your nursery and local area honey bee amicable. It's additionally essential that we convince the public authority to make a move. Join the age that protects the existence of honey bees.

Honey Bees Are Critical to the World's Economy

What did you have for breakfast today? Honey candy with a beverage? Flame-broiled tomatoes? Perhaps natural espresso? It's enticing to think honey bees simply furnish us with nectar, yet indeed they're behind a large part of the food we eat, including most products of the soil.

Honey bees are vital to our economy – without them, it would cost the world farmers billions of bucks every year to fertilize yields. In a world without honey bees, our food would cost much more to create and our economy wouldn't endure.

A Solid Climate Needs Honey Bees

Regardless of your perspective about honey bees, whether you feel they are enchanting or irritating, honey bees are unfathomably significant. They fertilize plants in nurseries, natural flowers in amusement parks, and the more extensive open country, including more than 3/4 of the world's wildflowers. Prospering nature and sound creature populaces are an indication of how solid our current circumstance is, yet usually existing species face annihilation daily, including over 20,000 types of the honeybee and a fourth of UK vertebrates. Do whatever you can within your capacity to forestall mass termination and ensure the preservation of this beautiful creature and the climate.

Honey Bee Amicable Spaces Are Useful For Us As Well

Spots that are useful for pollinators are useful for individuals as well. We share honey bees' requirements for different, regular green spaces and the basics such places give, for example, clean air and water. They're significant in case we will adapt to a changing environment – normal spaces ingest overabundance water and heat, and can offer cool shade.

Honey Bees Are Artistic Symbols

From bar signs and town names, from Shakespeare to JK Rowling, from colony hair-dos to phrases like "having a bee in your bonnet" – the honey bee has been a star for quite a long time. Roman logician Pliny alluded to nectar as "the perspiration of the sky and the spit of the stars", while Middle age creator and artist Chaucer was one of the first to utilize the expression "occupied as honey bees".

The honey bee has consistently been a wellspring of uncommon enjoyment as a result of its corpulent highlights and textured base. Mr. Blunder in Oliver Contort and Dumbledore (a Cornish word for honey bee) in Harry Potter suit their names well.

Various Honey Bees Have Various Characters

The Bumblebee is presumably the most popular honey bee around, yet more than 270 types of honey bees have been recorded in some parts of the world. Bumblebees and honey bees live socially, drove by a sovereign, and overhauled by male robots and female working drones.

Lone honey bees will in general be more modest, and their nuclear family is comprised of a solitary pair. Albeit heaps of lone honey bees can be found in one territory, they work alone. Honey bees are recognized by their enormous hairy bodies and species incorporate the dark and-yellow striped Nursery honey bee and Red-followed honey bee. Lone honey bees incorporate artisan honey bees, leaf-shaper honey bees, and mining honey bees. The Fleece carder honey bee takes hair from plants to weave its home, while the Red artisan honey bee lives inside empty plant stems and openings in wood

Imperiled Honey Bee Species

For decades, some part of the world has lost 13 types of the honey bee, and a further 35 species are considered under danger of eradication. None are ensured by law. Across Europe almost 1 out of 10 wild honey bee species faces termination.

What Are The Reasons For Honey Bee Decay?

We realize enough to plan something for help, regardless of whether a few issues may require more exploration to be completely perceived. Known reasons for honey bee decrease incorporate things that influence us as well. These remember changes for land use, living space misfortune, illness, pesticides, cultivating rehearses, contamination, intrusive non-local plant and creature species, and environmental change.

Without Honey Bees, We're In A Tough Situation

The viewpoint for honey bees right presently is very grim – and their drop in numbers is an indication of the situation of the regular world. Across most of the world, we regularly underestimate nature and how it helps us. Truly, on the off chance that we need an economy that accommodates everybody's necessities in the long haul, we need to care for our regular habitat. Our legislators need to comprehend the significance of securing the common world – including honey bees.

Honey bees and pesticides

There's currently overpowering logical proof that pesticides hurt honey bees. Pesticides are chemicals farmers regularly utilized for cultivating. The European Sanitation Authority (EFSA) proclaimed in 2013 that they represented an "inadmissible danger" to honey bees, prompting impermanent limitations.

Also, in April 2018 nations across the European Association – including the UK – cast a ballot to boycott the open-air utilization of 3 honey bee hurting pesticides. We need the UK government to keep any EU limitations on honey bee hurting pesticides post-Brexit.

Together we can boycott honey bees hurting pesticides for great so honey bees can flourish.

Honey bees are not difficult to help

You can have a gigantic effect where you reside by doing a couple of basic things. Planting blossoms wealthy in nectar will truly help honey bees discover the food they need. Picking neighborhood, English nectar will loan your help to our bumblebees and their beekeepers. Empowering your companions and neighbors to do a similar will help make honey bee amicable networks.

Honey bees are urgent in the open country. However, they're fundamental in the city as well. A wild window confines the center of the metropolitan wilderness has extraordinary worth. An entire structure canvassed in window boxes is considerably more valuable and looks fabulous.

You can get honey bee agreeable plants!

If you've chosen to improve some place for honeybees, the primary activity is to study your spot. Go for a short stroll to perceive what's pulling in honey bees – are there plants or trees that look especially well known? Heaps of elaborate blossoms have been reared to contain no nectar – they may look great however do little for untamed life.

Honey bees love spices

Pick blossoms with dust that honey bees can get at effectively – single-bloom assortments for instance. Grow a scope of plants that will give a progression of blossoms to as far as might be feasible during the year – honey bees need nectar from late-winter until late-fall. The extraordinary thing about planting is that it's useful for you just as natural life. Outside air and delicate exercise improve wellbeing and prosperity. The size of your honey bee cordial development will rely upon your external space, yet everything makes a difference. On the off chance that you don't have a nursery, plant a window box or hanging crate. You could attempt:

Blooming spices – marjoram, chives, sage, and thyme.

Low cultivators – crocus, bluebell, snowdrop, and nasturtium.

Rugged plants – hyssop, hebe, rosemary, and lavender.

Trees – hawthorn, hazel, holly, and willow.

Products of the soil – strawberries, tomatoes, and beans

Appealing ornamentals – achillea, allium, angelica, echinacea, foxglove, and verbena.

Single honey bees need singular homes

There are more than 200 types of singular honey bee that need singular homes. A few animal types burrow into the ground, sandy banks, or disintegrating mortar. Others utilize empty stems or openings in the wood. By making things like this accessible it's not difficult to make ideal convenience for lone honey bees. You could give a heap of empty plant stems or a lavish honey bee inn, loaded with dry logs, untreated wood, and delicate, brittle mortar. The other thing honey bees need is water – so ensure there's a source close by like a water basin or lake, particularly on hot days.

Neighborhood nectar is ideal

A simple – and scrumptious – approach to help the English bumble bee is to purchase its rewards for so much hard work: uphold beekeepers by picking nectar delivered close to you. You'll see all the various tones nectar can be – from dull green and profound gold to practically unadulterated white. What's more, it very well may be a pardon to purchase different items like nectar lager, beeswax candles, and sweet-smelling nectar cleansers and ointments.

Figure out How Honey bees Make Nectar

Before you hop in and begin requesting supplies, how about you make a stride back and see precisely how a hive function and what honey bees do.

Honey bees make homes in nature, fly to blossoms and concentrate nectar, at that point take the nectar back to the hive and brush, where it gradually gets the nectar.

Interface With Nearby Beekeeping Associations

In beekeeping, a few subtleties can be explicit to your neighborhood. The idea of beekeeping implies that you'll be best if you have solid nearby assets to draw on: somebody to come to check your hive or help you discover your sovereign if necessary, for instance. Connect and locate your nearby beekeeping affiliation and go to gatherings. A few affiliations offer guides that can be significant in encouraging you during your first season.

CHAPTER TWO

BEEHIVE

How to Set Up Your Beehive

To keep honey bees, you need an apiary. In the wild, honey bees construct their hive, normally in an empty tree trunk or another protected spot, however, it tends to be anyplace. As a terrace beekeeper, you will give a man-created hive to your honey bees so you can help keep up the state and effectively gather the nectar. There are a couple of various decisions for the patio or bigger scope beekeeper. Langstroth and top-bar hives are the most normally discovered sorts.

Find out About Beekeeping Assignments

What is associated with dealing with your honey bees? Similar to planting, beekeeping undertakings are best separated by the season. The best ideal opportunity to begin your hive is in the spring so the settlement you start with has the opportunity to develop, lay brood (child honey bees), increment in number, and store nectar before the colder time of year sets in.

CHAPTER THREE

BEEKEEPING SUPPLIES

Assemble Your Beekeeping Supplies

What do you need to truly begin beekeeping? Find out about the fundamental supplies and what you can manage without for the present. Keep in mind: start little, so you can make changes on the off chance that you alter your perspective later. A few supplies are better-bought face to face, while others can be requested online.

How to Gather Your Beekeeping Supplies

Request Your Bumblebees

Whenever you've assembled your provisions and amassed a lot of beekeeping information, it's an ideal opportunity to arrange your honey bees! You will probably arrange what is classified as "bundle honey bees" and a sovereign, or a "nuc province." Of the two, a nuc settlement is a more settled arrangement of honey bees with a sovereign who has just begun brooding. It can give your hive a great start in case you're ready to get one.

CHAPTER FOUR

BEEKEEPING HIVE SYSTEM

At the point when you are beginning in beekeeping, perhaps the main decision is the sort of colony of bees you'll utilize. There are a few sorts, and your decision ought to be deliberately made since your decision will include a venture of cash just as an interest in learning the procedures for that specific strategy for beekeeping. Most starting beekeepers will select between a Langstroth-style hive and a top-bar hive, yet an inexorably well-known structure is the Warré hive, a changed, vertical form of the top-bar plan. Whatever style you decide to start your leisure activity, it's a smart thought to begin little, so that on the off chance that you choose to move techniques, you will not have squandered a lot of cash or exertion.

Ten-Frame Langstroth Hive

The stacked white boxes that the vast majority imagine when they consider beekeeping is called Langstroth hives, a style created by the Reverend Lorenzo Lorraine Langstroth (1810 to 1895), a local of Philadelphia, in 1851. This plan comprises square boxes stacked on each other and beats by a defensive, vented rooftop. The base levels are boxes organized to permit agonizing space for the honey bees, while the upper boxes are organized to hold wooden casings for the honey bees to load up with brush and nectar. This style is classified as "ten-outline" because the inside of each hive contains ten casings for holding nectar.

Advantages

1. Supplies and enlightening help are not difficult to track down.

2. This is an incredible framework where the greatest nectar creation is wanted.

3. This is the most well-known framework and thought about the all-inclusive beekeeping standard.

4. Most "old-school" beekeepers and business beekeepers utilize this style, and the strategies have culminated over numerous years.

Disadvantages

1. Working makes more disturbance for the hive.

2. The edges are hefty, each gauging as much as 60 pounds.

3. The cell size may cause health problems for the honey bees.

4. The framework is massive, and beekeepers end up keeping additional parts.

5. Beekeepers may have to smoke honey bees to quiet them enough to work with them.

Eight-Frame Langstroth Hive

Eight-outline hives work actually like the ten-outline Langstroth hives regarding structure, however, each container is marginally more modest, holding just eight edges rather than ten. What's the significance here? At the point when you lift a medium super hive loaded with nectar, it will weigh just around 30 pounds, rather than 60 pounds for a ten-outline medium super.

Advantages

1. Lighter and simpler to work with.

2. Same advantages as a ten-outline Langstroth hive, natural arrangement to the extent boxes and outlines.

Disadvantages

1. Parts are not exchangeable with ten-outline gear.

2. The framework is still moderately exceptional, and supplies might be harder to track down.

Top-Bar Hive

Top-bar hives are getting better known with patio aficionados and maintainable ranchers. It is the most established and most ordinarily utilized style on the planet. In this plan, a bunch of level bars is set across a box molded hive secured by a pivoted or removable cover, and honey bees assemble their brush descending from these bars, an extremely characteristic action. There are no edges utilized, and no establishment needed to keep the hive level. The bars are normally straightforward wooden wedges or strips that slide into openings to guarantee they hang straight. A top-bar hive is genuinely simple to construct yourself, albeit business top-bar hives are accessible. In more detailed variants of this style, the agonizing zone for the honey bees is set up by a divider board that limits the initial 8 to 10 bars nearby the kickoff of the hive, where the honey bees enter and exit. As the province develops, and brush and nectar fill the bars, the divider board is moved along the side and more bars are added. The gathering involves just lifting out the bars whenever they are covered with a nectar-filled brush.

Advantages

1. This is a generally economical type of beekeeping.

2. This plan is reasonable for individuals with inabilities or versatility issues.

3. Working is less problematic to honey bees—you needn't bother with smoke or a full honey bee suit.

4. The plan permits the honey bees to make a brush with a characteristic shape and cell size.

5. The hive is light and simple to work with.

6. The bars are light and simple to eliminate for assessment and reaping.

Disadvantages

1. The honey bees can die in chilly winters.

2. Brushes can sever or shape inappropriately.

3. Ventilation can be poor if the hive isn't constructed as expected.

4. You may experience difficulty discovering nearby help for this sort of beekeeping.

Warré Hive

A Warré hive is now and again depicted as a top-bar hive that is set up vertically. This style, created in France by Emile Warré (1867 to 1951), utilizes a heap of little, square hive boxes that have top bars instead of casings to hold the brush. There is typically no establishment with this style of the hive. It additionally utilizes an interesting style of hive cover: a blanket loaded up with sawdust or wood shaving, and a vented, calculated rooftop. This should give unrivaled dampness to the executives, as the sawdust-filled blanket ingests dampness that would then be able to escape utilizing the rooftop.

In this style, the honey bees assemble brush from the top bars descending into each container. As more space is required, extra boxes can be added to the lower part of the hive. In this way, the upper boxes are the first to load up with nectar. Warré hives are intended for insignificant reviews by the beekeeper. You can't eliminate bars for examination in a customary Warré hive because as the honey bees fabricate brush, they join it to within the hive dividers. The depression size is intended to permit the honey bees to burn-through their colder time of year stores all the more effectively and the general plan is intended to keep the honey bees hotter in cool environments.

Collecting involves eliminating upper boxes once they are brimming with nectar. Honey bees are permitted to get away or are eliminated from the open box, at that point the brush is removed from the bars and the nectar squeezed out. Collecting is done in later summer or tumble to guarantee the crates are full and that agonizing honey bees have moved to bring down boxes. Albeit, these hives are not as regular as Langstroth or even top-bar hives, they are encountering a resurgence in ubiquity, particularly among specialist beekeepers that need to get things done in a more "characteristic" way.

Advantages

1. Negligible investigations are required.

2. The establishment of less framework is more normal for honey bees.

3. The framework is interesting to those keen on more regular styles of beekeeping.

4. The size and state of the hive are more normal for honey bees, giving better overwintering and utilization of stores.

Disadvantages

1. The top bars can't be taken out for investigation of the hive.

2. This plan is Illegal in certain states (some state laws require mobile brush hives).

3. The framework doesn't utilize the standard gear utilized in different styles of beekeeping.

4. Since the framework is to some degree extraordinary, data on the

most proficient method to deal with the hives might be hard to get a hold of.

How to Choose The Right Hive System

The starting beekeeper would be astute to renounce the conversations over which "box" is better or more "normal" for keeping honey bees and spotlight rather on their comprehension of honey bee science. As such, if you need to be an effective beekeeper, you will be in an ideal situation learning the science of the honey bee – what honey bees do – and coupling that information with the honey bee's occasional propensities and regular senses. Understanding the exercises inside the hive is considerably more significant than the wooden box we house our honey bees in.

Some History

Before keeping honey bees, people burglarized honey bee settlements and frequently annihilated the hive while gathering that valued brilliant nectar we as a whole love. The absolute best records of humanity moving from chasing for honey bees and their nectar to starting to keep honey bees, come from Egypt. In Egypt, extended mud pots were utilized to hive honey bees. Afterward, hives of plug and wood were utilized, notwithstanding topsy turvy woven bushels called skeps. It isn't known precisely when honey bees were brought to the U.S., yet they are not local to North America. It is referred to that honey bees were brought here as ahead of schedule as the 1600s. Among the kinds of a colony in like manner use today, it's heartbreaking the Langstroth hive is frequently peered downward on once in a while essentially as a result of its relationship with business beekeeping. In the 1800s the dad of present-day beekeeping, Rev. Lorenzo Langstroth, made some significant disclosures, the best of which was presumably the revelation of honey bee space.

Honey bee space is roughly 3/eighth of an inch and is simply the room honey bees leave to move openly about the hive. Spaces less than that are regularly occupied with propolis and spaces bigger used to fabricate brush. This agreement considered the advancement of the portable casing which reformed beekeeping. The rule of honey bee space is applied taking all things together sorts of apiary today and appropriate brush dispersing is a significant plan issue.

What's a Bee Looking For in a Home?

In examinations directed by Tom Sealy in the woodlands close to Cornell University, he found that most settlements settled in trees with an opening no more noteworthy than two to five square inches. These openings were generally found on the south side of the tree close to the lower part of the tree pit. The normal home cavity had an all-out volume of around 41 quarts. In any case, bumblebees are truly versatile and are frequently found in structures, perch rooms, old tires, void boxes, rough cleft, and even give in. The key is the size of the hole, the size of the opening, and the area of the passage. (Pointing toward the south or east)

The present bee colonies coordinate the vast majority of the attributes found in wild honey bee states and are more extensive as well. They give (and honey bees require) a little passageway that is faultless, a dim nook shielded from the climate and space to fabricate sufficient equal brush to raise brood and store the stores important to see the state through the colder time of year.

Hive Maintainance

Bumblebees, alongside other pollinating bugs, are significant to the cultivation business and the imperativeness of our nurseries. Accordingly, an ever-increasing number of mortgage holders are deciding to keep up their bee colonies. An essential piece of a solid and maintainable beekeeping practice includes assessing the bee colony. The interaction should be led consistently, however not so regularly that it upsets the daily practice of the hive. For starting beekeepers, an assessment each seven to 10 days during spring and summer is a decent objective. Reviewing more than week after week will make your honey bees despondent by disturbing hive movement and hampering them daily.

The examination is best directed on a tolerably warm, dry day—over 60 degrees Fahrenheit. Dodge wet, cold days for examinations.

The Inspection Process

A standard bee colony comprises a progression of stacked boxes, some of which are expected to hold nectar for assortment, others that contain the brood province. An upper box holding nectar is frequently known as a nectar super, while a lower box holding the brood province passes by a few names, including brood box, profound super, profound box, or profound. Between the nectar supers and the brood boxes, there might be a level screen known as the sovereign excluder, however, this isn't found on all hives. This part is intended to keep the sovereign zeroed in on multiplication while working drones fill the nectar supers with nectar.

Investigating a colony of bees is the cycle of deliberately smoking and eliminating each crate until you arrive at the base layer, at that point cautiously reviewing the casings inside the cases and noticing what you see before reassembling the hive.

Readiness

To prepare for an examination, wear your honey bee suit or coat and shroud. Assemble your smoker and hive instrument. If you will top off feeders during the investigation, have them prepared. Light the smoker and sit tight for it to siphon out decent, cool smoke for the honey bees.

What You'll Need

- Tools
- Honey bee suit
- Smoker
- Hive apparatus
- Materials
- Notebook
- Directions

Open the Hive

Direct smoke by the passage before the hive, to befuddle the gatekeeper honey bees. Lift the external cover marginally and direct a couple of puffs of smoke under it. Allow the cover to withdraw delicately and hang tight for one to two minutes for the smoke to produce results.

Fun Fact

Individuals frequently say smoke "quiets" the honey bees, however, what it truly does is impart a sign that there is a fire close by, which makes them naturally gorge on nectar. While they're pigging out, they're not stressing over the huge, white-fit creature that is meddling with them. At the point when you see their heads line up at the top bars, seeing you, it's the ideal opportunity for more smoke.

Eliminate the Outer Cover

Eliminate the hive's external cover and painstakingly put it on the ground topsy turvy. Direct some smoke into the opening in the internal cover, on the off chance that you have one. Trust that the honey bees will respond to the smoke.

Eliminate the Inner Cover

Utilize your hive apparatus to tenderly pry up the inward cover and eliminate it. On the off chance that there is wax or propolis on the internal cover, utilize your hive apparatus to scratch it off. Set the inward cover on top of the external cover on the ground, being mindful so as not to harm any honey bees.

Eliminate the Honey Super

Pry up the top box—the nectar super—utilizing your hive device. Takeoff the super and set it on top of the internal cover. The nectar super can be a shallow, medium, or profound box.

If the hive has a second nectar super, smoke and eliminates this container, too. If the hive has a sovereign excluder situated beneath the nectar supers, eliminate it with the hive device and put it in a safe spot.

Note: Young provinces may not yet need nectar super. If yours doesn't have one, continue down to the profound boxes holding the province.

Smoke the Second Deep Box

Tenderly puff smoke into the following hive box. This is known as the subsequent profound, which in many hives is one of two boxes that hold the brood province. On the off chance that you have three medium boxes rather than two deeps, you'll simply rehash this twice until you get to the base box. You will begin your review with the base box.

Smoking the subsequent profound.

Eliminate the subsequent profound and spot it delicately on top of the nectar super or inward cover. You will investigate this container later.

Eliminating the subsequent profound.

Start your review with the primary (base) profound box. Direct smoke in the middle of the casings, at that point, eliminate the primary edge and set it either in a casing holder or delicately on top of the other hive boxes or the internal cover, taking consideration not to harm any honey bees.

Assess the Frames

Each in turn, cautiously pry each casing free utilizing your hive instrument, at that point lift up the casing and investigate it:

Attempt to recognize the sovereign.

This is simpler if she's stamped, yet it's as yet conceivable if she isn't. Search for her long, thin, unstriped mid-region and a circle of laborers around her. If you can't discover the sovereign, it's essential to discover eggs, which demonstrate the sovereign was there in the previous one to three days.

Check for any parasites or bugs—vermin, wax moth hatchlings, foulbrood, and so forth

Decide the number of casings is drawn out—loaded up with search prepared for nectar. At the point when seven of 10 casings are attracted to the base profound box, it's an ideal opportunity to add the subsequent profound box.

At the point when seven of 10 are attracted the subsequent profound, add a nectar super. On the off chance that the nectar super is near full, add another.

Check for Larvae

Part of examining the casings is searching for brood—covered and uncapped hatchlings and eggs. Appeared here is a lovely example of creating, uncapped hatchlings—this is the thing that you're searching for in your bee colony assessment.

Search for Eggs

Recognizing eggs is the main piece of the bee colony review for the new beekeeper, however, novices regularly discover the eggs hard to spot. Eggs look like slight grains of rice. There ought to be one for every cell, laid in the middle. If you have more than one egg for every cell, your hive has laying working drones—counsel an accomplished beekeeper about the present circumstance.

The most ideal approach to see eggs is to hold the casing shifted up toward the sky at around a 30-degree point, with the brilliant sun sparkling behind you. Hold it somewhat to the side of you so the shadow example of a cross-section from your cloak doesn't dark the eggs.

Utilizing understanding glasses or an amplifying glass can likewise help. You can shift the edge to and fro and try different things with the point of the sun and the casing until you see them. The base focus of the casing is normally the best spot to decidedly distinguish eggs.

Supplant the Frames

As you review each casing, put it out from the shadows space left by the past outline you eliminated. Push each edge facing the one before it as you supplant it—tenderly, to try not to harm any honey bees. Utilizing a honey bee brush or smoke helps move the honey bees far removed, particularly at the casing ears, where they are probably going to get squeezed.

Investigate the casings altogether, and don't change their request during an assessment. At the point when you get to the last casing, push the entire arrangement of edges together as one single unit, utilizing your hive instrument to make space in the front for the main edge. As you supplant the primary edge, utilize your hive apparatus to even up the space on one or the other side of the first and last edges with the goal that the arrangement of casings is focused in the container.

Supplant the Second Deep and Honey Super

With the main profound box assessed, continue to the subsequent profound box, reviewing the edges, and afterward restacking the container onto the principal profound box. Supplant the sovereign excluder, if your hive has one, supplant the nectar super. To do this, position the case with the edge on the back edge of the hive, at that point gradually "demolish" it forward, moving gradually to try not to harm any honey bees. You can utilize the smoker or honey bee brush to tenderly move the honey bees far removed.

Supplanting the subsequent profound

Slide on the internal cover utilizing the tractor strategy: Start toward one side and gradually slide the cover across the crate. Utilize the smoker or honey bee brush to move honey bees far removed, depending on the situation.

Supplant the outer cover

Tenderly supplant the external cover on the hive. At last, record your perceptions in your honey bee scratchpad or diary. Do this immediately because it's too simple to even consider forgetting the specific date and the subtleties of the investigation. Eliminate your suit, and set aside your smoker where it can wear out securely

CHAPTER FIVE

ORDER YOUR HONEY BEES

Whenever you've accumulated your provisions and amassed a lot of beekeeping information, it's an ideal opportunity to arrange your honey bees! You will probably arrange what is classified as "bundle honey bees" and a sovereign, or a "nuc province." Of the two, a nuc state is a more settled arrangement of honey bees with a sovereign who has effectively begun laying brood. It can give your hive a head start in case you're ready to get one.

How to Order Your Honey Bees

At the point when you start a beekeeping activity, requesting the honey bees is the last advance. You have numerous on the web and mail-request destinations to look over. You can arrange to bundle honey bees or nucs from the vast majority of these sources, yet you ought to likewise check with your neighborhood beekeeping relationship since it is in some cases simpler and more affordable to acquire your honey bees from nearby sources. A nuc is a more modest, core state of honey bees when contrasted with a full hive.

It is ideal to arrange your honey bees in the colder time of year for shipment in March through May. Here and there bundle honey bees sell out, so stay away from issues by requesting early.

Discover more about the absolute best online honey bee providers who will deliver honey bees to you; numerous additionally have honey bees accessible for pickup. There are a lot more providers who have sites, however, a portion of these may not transport the honey bees, necessitating that you get them yourself.

Draper's Super Bee Apiaries Inc.

Draper's is situated in Pennsylvania and sells bundle honey bees and sovereigns just as a choice of beekeeping supplies. They now and then have nucs accessible for pick up as it were. They offer Italian, Italian/Russian, Carniolan, and Minnesota Hygienic Carniolan subspecies of honey bees.

Kelley Bees

Kelley Bees, situated in Clarkson, Kentucky, has been doing business since 1924. This organization sells Italian and Russian bundle honey bees and beekeeping supplies like casings, hive packs to amass, defensive garments, traps, baits, and extraction supplies.

Long Lane Honey Bee Farms

Long Lane Honey Bee Farms is a privately-owned company situated in Illinois, which sells nucs just as bundle honey bees. They additionally offer honey bees as a feature of their fledgling beekeeping units. Supplies incorporate hives, instruments and smokers, defensive garments, sovereign raising hardware, and nectar extraction gear.

Rossman Apiaries, LLC

Since 1936 Rossman Apiaries in Georgia has been a privately-owned company that sells bundle honey bees, sovereigns, and beekeeping supplies and hardware including hives made of cypress wood. They offer enhancements, taking care of provisions, devices and smokers, and beekeeping books.

NetWeaver Apiaries

NetWeaver is another privately-owned company; this one traces back to

1888. The organization sells bundle honey bees, sovereigns, and reproducer sovereigns for the beekeeper who needs to raise their sovereigns. They are situated in Austin, Texas, however, transport everywhere in the United States. Their BeeWeaver sovereigns are a mix of Buckfast, BeeSMaRT, and AllStar lines and are reared to be impervious to varroa bugs, have high nectar creation, and produce solid provinces.

B and B Honey Farm

B and B Honey Farm sells bundle honey bees, sovereigns, and a wide scope of beekeeping supplies. Established in 1975 in Houston, Minnesota, B and B Honey Farm at first sold honey bees in a restricted provincial region, yet now ships to any purchaser in USDA strength zones two to five. This incorporates New England and the northern Midwest; then again, this avoids California and the majority of the southern portion of the U.S.

Sweet Mountain Honey

Situated in upper east Georgia, Sweet Mountain Honey has some expertise in Italian bundle honey bees, and boats to 30 states in the U.S. Sweet Mountain Honey sells bundle honey bees and sovereigns, nucs, just as hives and different supplies.

How to Maintain Queenright Colony

Each spring, you should re-sovereign my most grounded hives to diminish amassing. A province is more averse to the crowd when the sovereign's pheromones are solid, and the pheromones are most grounded in a first-year sovereign. Indeed, as per most sources, another sovereign is the absolute best hindrance to amassing. Be that as it may, it appears to be ludicrous to take your absolute best sovereigns, execute them, and supplant them with others. Also, if the new sovereign is dismissed, you are left with nothing.

Keep those sovereigns as opposed to executing them. To do this, eliminate the sovereign alongside an edge of brood and an edge of nectar and put them in a two-outline nuc. At that point, bring the new sovereign into the hive. If anything turns out badly with the new sovereign, you can generally once again introduce the former one, or on the other hand, you can keep her "for possible later use" for some other reason.

For instance, a new supply may give an impression of being queenless. The multitude constructed brush in which it put away possibly nectar, filter the honey bees through a sovereign excluder, If you'd did not see any queen, take one of your saved sovereigns and present her. When she begins laying the settlement will likely supplant her, however without her to kick things off, the entire multitude would pass on.

At the point when I previously began saving sovereigns, I thought about what I would do when the two-outline nucs got excessively crowded. However, I tracked down that these little settlements will in general grow to occupy the accessible space and afterward stay steady. At the point when you consider the big picture, they aren't adequately large to crowd or even to steal away. So they simply stay little. In the past, I've kept these "save" sovereigns the entire summer.

Here and there I just put a multitude of the cell, brood, and nectar in the little nucs. It appears to take everlastingly, however, the honey bees ultimately produce a laying sovereign and I simply leave her there. On the off chance that one doesn't succeed, I simply start another. Since I'm utilizing her just as reinforcement, it doesn't matter how long it requires.

CHAPTER SIX

INTRODUCE BEES TO THE HIVE

Presently comes the pleasant part! Your honey bees have shown up, and it's an ideal opportunity to set up the hive and get them settled. You need to securely and serenely acquaint the honey bees with their new home. At that point, pause for a moment and let them get comfortable while you notice the comings and goings. Such a lot of fun!

How to Introduce Bees to the Hive

Bundles of honey bees are containers uncommonly worked to transport honey bees securely and safely. These bundles are sold by the heaviness of the honey bees, with about 3,000 to 5,000 honey bees for each pound. Most bundles range from two to five pounds and usually accompany a sovereign except if in any case determined.

What do I need to begin?

Putting a feeder confine another honey bee hive before you get your bundle of honey bees, be certain you have all the fitting hardware prepared. This incorporates a hive stand, screened base, single profound hive body with 10 wooden edges, and an establishment with a passage reducer and feeder introduced.

Make certain to set up the parts in the area you wish to keep your hive. Different materials that will make setting up your hive simpler incorporate a splash bottle loaded up with sugar water (pre-blended at a 1:1 proportion), a hive device, and a wood screw or other sharp instrument to help eliminate the plugin the sovereign enclosure.

Parts of a Package

Splashing down bundle honey bees Packages of honey bees are regularly made with a wood casing, top and base, and wire screen sides. The wooden cover holds a metal can feeder loaded up with sugar water for the honey bees to eat while on the way. Inside the bundle, you will likewise discover a wood or plastic sovereign pen. This holds the sovereign securely isolated from the laborers while they get familiar with her aroma.

Before you start, fog the honey bees with sugar water to help quiet them. To ensure you fog every one of the honey bees in the bundle, you may have to delicately bump the honey bees by tapping the bundle on the ground. Be mindful so as not to over-wet the honey bees, particularly on cool days.

You are presently prepared to start introducing the bundle.

Opening the highest point of bundle honey bees with a hive device. With your hive collected and the cover eliminated, pull out and put to the side three or four edges from the center to make a space for your new honey bees. Then, eliminate the wooden cover from the bundle with your hive apparatus, uncovering the metal that can be used to take care of the honey bees during transportation. Eliminate the lash holding the sovereign pen, being mindful so as not to allow the confine to fall into the bundle.

Spot the bundle on its side over the space in the new hive where you eliminated the four edges and delicately slide out the metal can.

Tip: Add the leftover sugar water in the metal can into the passage feeder.

Moving honey bees from the bundle into the hive. Gently pull the sovereign pen out of the bundle and set it out of the way on top of the casing. Flip around the bundle and tenderly shake it to help the honey bees fall into the hive. You may have to strike the side of the bundle to help move the honey bees into the hive.

Tip: Don't stress over getting every honey bee out of the bundle. When most honey bees are in the hive, place the open bundle close to the front of the hive to urge any excess honey bees to enter.

Introducing the Queen

It's presently an ideal opportunity to introduce the sovereign. We propose leaving the sovereign in her enclosure for the initial not many days so the laborers have the opportunity to get acclimated with her pheromones. There are a few ways to do this:

In some sovereign pens, a stopper covers a white sweets plug that keeps the sovereign in the enclosure until the honey bees eat through the treats and delivery her. Utilize a wood screw or other sharp apparatus to deliberately eliminate the plug and uncover the sweets.

In other sovereign confines, there is no treats plug behind the stopper. For this situation leave the fixed sovereign confine in the hive for a couple of days before resuming the hive and delicately eliminating the plug.

Tip: If your sovereign confine doesn't have a treats plug, you can utilize a scaled-down marshmallow to plug the opening after eliminating the stopper. The laborers will gradually eat through the marshmallow and delivery the sovereign.

Examining outlines in another honey beehive. Once you have arranged the sovereign pen, place it between two casings and utilize the pressing factor of the edges to hold the sovereign enclosure set up.

At last, supplant the casings you eliminated in sync one. Try to keep appropriate dispersing between the casings, and supplant the hive cover.

Congrats, you did it! Following seven days, verify whether the sovereign has been delivered from the enclosure or delivered her physically. This is additionally a decent and ideal opportunity to check the establishment and if the sovereign has begun to lay.

How to Keep Your Bees Healthy and Happy

Step by step, season via season, honey bees need continuous consideration. Yet, they don't need tremendous time speculation. You should mind them to some degree regularly, however, perception is a decent level of how you'll deal with keeping your honey bees cheerful. Simply watching hive action can be unwinding and enlightening. You can coordinate beekeeping errands by the season, from setting the honey bees up in spring to reaping nectar, to setting up the hive for winter.

How to Control Overcrowding

Amassing is bees natural means of increasing in numbers

Bumblebees' common methods for expanding is to the crowd and when they swarm the province gets ready around 12 sovereign cells on the base edge of the crowding. Also, around two days before the sovereign cells incubate which is 16 days after the sovereign laid the egg. The hive is probably going to part down the middle and multitude.

Outer signs that bees are likely to swarm

The outer signs that honey bees are probably going to crowd is shown by the trip of the honey bee so if there's a ton of trip of honey bees it's a sign the province is solid and especially if the honey bees are going across the entire width of your passage. So if you see you need to peer inside the hive to search for the presence that the honey bees might be amassing. The sign is around 12 sovereign cells on the base edge of the brooding outline.

In this hive here there's a ton of action so the hive is probably going to crowd the honey bees additionally will frequently hang up the front of the hive in incredible numbers because there's inadequate space for them to all get inside the settlement so that is a sign your honey bees are amassing and they should be checked.

Honey bees returning exhausted from the field

The honey bees that we're presently noticing are honey bees that have returned with food. They've flown a reasonable way, and they're genuinely depleted. So because they're depleted they've arrived at the front of the province before strolling into the settlement. This is an indication of a nectar stream or a dust stream that is truly extraordinary in spring. Furthermore, this regularly occurs in spring where honey bees stroll into the settlement.

Signs of overcrowding

On the off chance that we look inside a province, we can tell if it's packed by eliminating the top and looking under the cover. Also, on the off chance that we look under the top in this province, we see many honey bees that is inactive and they're in the cover so that is a certain sign that the populace in this hive is genuinely solid. A sign the province may crowd in the spring.

Reviewing inside a strong colony in spring

On the off chance that we look further and eliminate the cover and we take a gander at the highest points of the casings, we can see honey bees are on each edge in this super and there're honey bees over the edges. On the off chance that I eliminate an edge, we can perceive what the state of this super resembles. This is presented toward the beginning of August (spring) so we can see from this casing there are a reasonable number of honey bees up in the super and the super has a decent stockpile of put away nectar and nectar. Nectar is in the open cells, nectar's in the covered cells.

Reviewing the brood box

So now we will peer inside a settlement in august that is genuinely solid and that conceivably may crowd in about September. Settlements ordinarily swarm more than once per year if they're not overseen appropriately. So we take the top off, puff under the top, set the top back on. At that point take the cover off and we'll see there're honey bees in the top. It's a sensibly solid province we'll take off the super and afterward, we can glance in the brood box.

We puff once more, lift the excluder off check there's no sovereign on the sovereign excluder, which there isn't. At that point, the second casing from the divider is normally the simplest one to take out with the hive instrument. So we take this out to take a gander at the brood home to perceive what the strength of the state is probably going to be. We haul that out cautiously like that and we notice that the second edge from the divider has effectively got drone cells in it. This means that honey bees are prosperous this season and might be going to the crowd is the proof of robot cells. So they are drone cells there, they're laborer cells. This shows the state is in magnificent condition for this season. We likewise note that this protein is dust put away in those cells. That is an indication that the settlement is in amazing condition this season and possibly could crowd in the following three or a month.

Noticing a dummy queen cell (also known as a play cup)

We'll presently analyze another casing, so I'll put that edge out of the province however not on the ground so we currently haul this edge out and we see this edge and we'll see barely out of interest there's what we call a spurious sovereign cell which is simply there that is not a multitude cell but rather if the state planned to crowd the honey bees will make their phones a sovereign cells along this base edge of the brush.

Arising of a newly born worker bee

If we look further and eliminate the cover and we take a gander at the highest points of the casings we can see honey bees are on each casing in this super and there are honey bees over the edges if I eliminate an edge we can perceive what the state of this super resembles and this is currently toward the beginning of August. We can see from this casing there are a reasonable number of honey bees up in the super and the super has a great inventory of put-away nectar and nectars in the open cells nectar's in the cap cells. Presently we will peer inside a settlement in august that is genuinely solid that possibly may crowd in about September. Settlements ordinarily swarm a few times per year if they're not overseen appropriately.

We take the top off puff under the cover set the top back on taking the top off and we'll see there are honey bees in the top so it's a sensibly solid province. We'll take off the super and afterward, we can glance in the brood box. We puff once more, lift the excluder off, check there's no sovereign on the sovereign excluder which there isn't. At that point, the second casing from the divider is typically the simplest one to take out with the hive instrument. So we take this out to take a gander at the brood home to perceive what the strength of the state is probably going to be.

Presence of drones in August (not long before springtime)

We haul that out cautiously, and we notice that the second edge from the divider has effectively got drone cells in it. So a sign that honey bees are prosperous this season and possibly going to crowd is the proof of robot cells so their robot cells there.

This shows the settlement is in amazing condition for this season we additionally note that this protein as dust put away in those phones there and that is an indication that the province is in incredible condition this season and conceivably could crowd in the following three or a month we'll presently analyze another casing so I'll put that casing out of the state yet not on the ground so we currently haul this casing out and we see this edge and we'll see barely out of interest there's what we call a fake sovereign cell which is simply there that is not a multitude cell but rather if the state planned to crowd the honey bees will make their own phones a sovereign cells along this base edge of the brush so they're probably going to put them there perhaps there and around 12 however in any casing in the brood box so you need to take a gander at each edge in the brood box to check whether your state's probably going to crowd for this situation here the honey bees have changed over a laborer cell into a sovereign cell that implies that the honey bees supplant their own sovereign or if the sovereign's been killed and they fabricate crisis cells they as of now use magma where they planned to supplant the sovereign by taking care of magma that would have been laborers override yourselves are worked as sovereign cells yet on the essence of the brush that way and there's generally just a single a few on that face like that so on this edge here which is the third one in from the divider we have great put away dust we have seal brood we have unlocked brood and we have what we call a spurious sovereign cell so if the hive planned to crowd that formed cell would be put on the lower part of the edge of the brush along here and they may assemble a few here a few in another casing a few in another edge until they get around 12 nut molded cells that subsequent to developing they incubate and the province will crowd the multitude typically withdraws a few days before the main sovereign cell hatches from the time the egg's laid the state will crowd a few days before it arises so it requires 16 days so the fourteenth day ahead the province may crowd yet that sovereign cell will be on that lower edge there and there'll be around 12 in the province so here we have a working drone going to arise that egg was laid 21 days prior it's covered brood here and here is put away dust which means that the state has a ton of protein in the hive since dust is protein another sign that provinces may crowd is the presence of robots in august and that honey bee there is a robot a male honey bee they don't sting so on the off chance that you see a ton of male honey bees this season it's likewise an indication of success and we saw a robot brood beforehand that hadn't brought forth yet this current one's as of now brought forth and that is a male honey bee so you see a ton of them in your settlement it's a sign the province may well need to crowd in the spring

CHAPTER SEVEN

INSPECT YOUR BEEHIVE

Honey bees, alongside other pollinating creepy crawlies, are critical to the agriculture business and the essentialness of our nurseries. Accordingly, an ever-increasing number of mortgage holders are deciding to keep up their colonies of bees. An essential piece of a sound and manageable beekeeping practice includes assessing the bee colony. The cycle should be directed consistently, yet not so frequently that it disturbs the daily schedule of the hive. For starting beekeepers, a review each seven to 10 days during spring and summer is a decent objective. Assessing more than week after week will make your honey bees troubled by disturbing hive movement and hindering them daily.

The investigation is best led on a modestly warm, dry day—over 60 degrees

Fahrenheit. Evade wet, cold days for examinations.

The Inspection Process

A standard bee colony comprises a progression of stacked boxes, some of which are planned to hold nectar for assortment, others that contain the brooding state. An upper box holding nectar is regularly known as a nectar super, while a lower box holding the brooding state passes by a few names, including brood box, profound super, profound box, or profound. Between the nectar supers and the brood boxes, there might be a level screen known as the sovereign excluder, however, this isn't found on all hives. This part is intended to keep the sovereign zeroed in on generation while working drones fill the nectar supers with nectar.

Assessing a colony of bees is the interaction of deliberately smoking and eliminating each crate until you arrive at the base layer, at that point cautiously examining the edges inside the containers and noticing what you see before reassembling the hive.

Planning

To prepare for an examination, wear your honey bee suit or coat and cloak. Accumulate your smoker and hive device. On the off chance that you will top off feeders during the assessment, have them prepared. Light the smoker and hang tight for it to siphon out decent, cool smoke for the honey bees.

What You'll Need

> Hardware/Tools

> Honey bee suit

> Smoker

> Hive instrument

Materials

- ➢ Scratchpad

- ➢ Guidelines

"Fun Fact"

Individuals frequently say smoke "quiets" the honey bees, yet what it truly does is impart a sign that there is a fire close by, which makes them intuitively gorge on nectar. While they're pigging out, they're not agonizing over the large, white-fit creature that is playing with them. At the point when you see their heads line up at the top bars, seeing you, it's the ideal opportunity for more smoke.

CHAPTER EIGHT

BEEKEEPING TASKS BY THE SEASON

Altogether yet the hottest environments, bumblebees follow an occasional example, and accordingly, the errands of the beekeeper likewise follow a schedule musicality. Beekeeping errands can be isolated by the season, however, you should remember that seasons in your specific locale may differ a smidgen from the scheduled dates. The beginning of "spring" in northern North Dakota, for instance, is well past March 21/22, and "summer" in Florida is an extensively longer season than Alaska's ten-week season. Keeping an eye on your honey bees regularly throughout it is a smart thought, however can be exaggerated. you would prefer not to upset their hive building and day by day exercises excessively.

Spring Tasks

Spring is certainly an opportunity to get new honey bees and start a hive! Peruse up in pre-spring on beekeeping, plan your hive, purchase or assemble it, and begin going to those nearby beekeeping clubs.

- ✓ Continue to take care of the honey bees if essential. They will have devoured the vast majority of their nectar stores over winter, and you should ensure they have food until sprouting roses are available to give nectar.

- ✓ Position an unfilled hive or two on the off chance that a portion of the honey bees swarm and are searching for new homes. On the off chance that you don't do this, you could lose honey bees that move somewhere else. Spring is when honey bees multitude and travel.

- ✓ Gather nectar from a setup hive: when blossoms are sprouting, collect any honeycomb not utilized over the colder time of year.

- ✓ Examine your hive for a strong brood design, and on the off chance that you presume the sovereign has passed on, supplant her.

- ✓ If you have more than one hive, even out the populaces so the quantity of honey bees is generally equivalent across your hives.

Summer Tasks

Throughout the mid-year your honey bees will fundamentally deal with themselves—you simply need to determine the status of them a long time and head off any issues before they swell into large issues.

✓ Quit taking care of now, as the honey bees will be in flight continually for nectar.

✓ Check regularly to ensure there are water sources close to your hives.

✓ Watch to ensure more grounded hives are not looting more vulnerable hives.

✓ Investigate regularly to ensure the sovereign is laying great.

✓ Screen for Varroa bug invasions.

✓ Ensure brushes are hanging straight in case you're utilizing foundationless or top bar techniques.

✓ Reap nectar.

Autumn Tasks

Presently it's pinnacle nectar assortment time, and an ideal opportunity for ensuring your honey bees are ready for winter.

✓ Gather nectar, yet try to leave enough for the honey bees for nourishment for winter.

✓ Check the example of the brushes, searching for great brood designs.

✓ Check for illnesses; treat or dispose of unhealthy brushes.

✓ Add powerless hives to more grounded ones, if there is sign of sans disease.

✓ Diminish the hive entrance, put on mouse watches, guarantee satisfactory ventilation. Complete any medicines for sicknesses and vermin.

✓ Start to take care of honey bees once-blooming plants and nectar are not, at this point accessible.

✓ Shield the hive from winter twists, yet take into account great ventilation.

✓   Weight down the highest points of the hives to monitor them against overturning in winter winds.

Winter Tasks

Before winter, you'll help your honey bee province get settled and cozy for the long virus spell ahead.

✓   Ensure all infection medicines are finished.

✓   Ensure the hives are shielded from the breeze.

✓   As winter hits, screen your hives for wind harm regularly, and check openings to ensure there is ventilation. Your honey bees can endure cold, yet fixing the hives completely can cause buildup that will pulverize the populace.

✓   As winter approaches spring mind them on hotter days by rapidly opening the highest point of the hive to ensure the honey bees have sufficient nectar for food. On the off chance that they are out of food, place dust patties or another type of food in the hive.

✓   Request new hardware and honey bees. Ordinarily, late February or early March is the most recent date you can make these orders on schedule for spring.

CHAPTER NINE

HONEY BEES FEEDING

You might be contemplating whether your bumblebees will starve or whether they have enough stores to endure the colder time of year. Also, you might need to urge your province to develop appropriately in the spring for ideal wellbeing. Anyway, when and how would you feed your honey bees?

When Do You Feed Bees?

In an ideal world, you'd leave the honey bees a lot of nectar and you would not have to take care of your bumblebees. Nonetheless, now and again there is a helpless nectar stream and the honey bees probably won't have sufficient nectar put away, particularly on the off chance that you have another province that was simply begun in the spring. If you can get your hive effectively, it very well may be light on nectar. Every state needs at any rate 50-60 pounds of put-away nectar to keep them from starvation in the colder time of year. On the off chance that you know early enough in the season, as in the fall, you can start taking care of them. Regardless of whether you don't take care of it until winter and late-winter, you can in any case take care of the honey bees. You should utilize granulated sugar or fondant during cold weather days.

Instructions to Feed Bees

You can utilize an assortment of kinds of feeders to take care of your honey bees, simply ensure that the sort you pick is fitting to the environment and the necessities of your honey bees. A few feeders work better compared to other people. A hive-top feeder made of a rearranged bucket for certain little openings punched in the focal point of the top functions admirably. Bricklayer containers can likewise be transformed along these lines.

If keeping an eye on or taking care of honey bees in winter, don't open the hive except if it is at any rate 40 degrees F outside with practically zero breezes. Never eliminate casings to investigate them except if it is at any rate 60 degrees F outside.

One thought when taking care of honey bees is whether you need to animate brood creation. A few types of feed animate brood creation more than others: for instance, granulated sugar doesn't as a result of its lower water content. Just feed as much as fundamental. Overloading can animate honey bees to crowd or overproduce brood.

On the off chance that you have nectar put away, you can take care of this back to your honey bees. Nectar is the best honey bee food. Be that as it may, never utilized bought nectar, since it can acquaint infections and pollution with your hive! Beekeepers in some cases put to the side dim, solidly shaded, or other "off" nectar to take care of honey bees in a crisis. Something else, make sugar syrup or feed dry sugar.

Dust Patties Feeding

Honey bees need protein, so you can likewise take care of them dust patties if essential. You can buy them or make them from dry powder. Spot the dust patty on the top bars. Dust is fundamental for late-winter brood raising, so in case you're stressed over your honey bees, use dust patties in late-winter.

Fondant and Sugar Candy Feeding

Fondant and sugar candy can be taken care of in winter on the off chance that it is excessively cold for sugar syrup and on the off chance that it is a crisis.

Sugar Candy: Add 12 pounds of sugar to a quart of bubbling water, blending admirably. Steer for 15 minutes, at that point, add 1/2 teaspoon salt and 1 teaspoon cream of tartar. Let cool fairly, at that point mix energetically and fill dishes. Once completely cooled, rearrange the dish over the edges holding the group. Make certain to likewise look at the hard sweets formula.

Fondant: Bring one quart of water to bubble in a huge pot. Mood killer heat, add 5 lb granulated sugar, and mix continually. Whenever sugar is broken up, carry water to bubble again and continue to mix. Carry blend to hardball treats stage, 260-270 degrees F on a sweets thermometer. Fill molds or onto treat sheets fixed with wax paper. Once cooled, break into more modest pieces and store in wax paper in the cooler.

CHAPTER TEN

HARVESTING

How to Open the Hive

Direct smoke by the passage before the hive, to confound the watchman honey bees. Lift the external cover somewhat and direct a couple of puffs of smoke under it. Allow the cover to withdraw tenderly and sit tight for one to two minutes for the smoke to produce results.

Eliminate the Outer Cover

Eliminate the hive's external cover and deliberately put it on the ground. Direct some smoke into the opening in the inward cover, if you have one. Trust that the honey bees will respond to the smoke.

Eliminate the Inner Cover

Utilize your hive instrument to delicately pry up the internal cover and eliminate it. On the off chance that there is wax or propolis on the inward cover, utilize your hive instrument to scratch it off. Set the internal cover on top of the external cover on the ground, being mindful so as not to harm any honey bees.

Eliminate the Honey Super

Pry up the top box—the nectar super—utilizing your hive apparatus. Takeoff the super and set it on top of the inward cover. The nectar super can be a shallow, medium, or profound box.

On the off chance that the hive has a second nectar super, smoke and eliminate in this case as well. On the off chance that the hive has a sovereign excluder situated underneath the nectar supers, eliminate it with the hive device and put it in a safe spot.

Note: Young states may not yet need nectar super. On the off chance that yours doesn't have one, continue down to the profound boxes holding the state.

Smoke the Second Deep Box

Tenderly puff smoke into the following hive box. This is known as the subsequent profound, which in many hives is one of two boxes that hold the brood province. On the off chance that you have three medium boxes rather than two deeps, you'll simply rehash this twice until you get to the base box. You will begin your investigation with the base box.

Eliminate the Second Deep Box

Eliminate the subsequent profound and spot it tenderly on top of the nectar super or internal cover. You will review this container later.

Eliminate the First Frame

Start your assessment with the main (base) profound box. Direct smoke in the middle of the edges, at that point, eliminate the primary edge and set it either in a casing holder or tenderly on top of the other hive boxes or on the inward cover, taking consideration not to harm any honey bees.

How to Remove Bees from the Hive

Each cautiously pry each casing free utilizing your hive apparatus, at that point lift the casing and examine it:

Attempt to recognize the sovereign. This is simpler if she's checked, yet it's as yet conceivable on the off chance that she isn't. Search for her long, thin, unstriped midsection and a circle of laborers around her. On the off chance that you can't discover the sovereign, it's critical to discover eggs, which demonstrate the sovereign was there in the previous one to three days.

Check for any parasites or irritations—bugs, wax moth hatchlings, foulbrood, and so on. Decide the number of edges is drawn out—loaded up with look over-prepared for nectar. At the point when seven of 10 edges are attracted to the base profound box, it's an ideal opportunity to add the subsequent profound box. At the point when seven of 10 are attracted the subsequent profound, add a nectar super. If the nectar super is near full, add another.

Check for Larvae

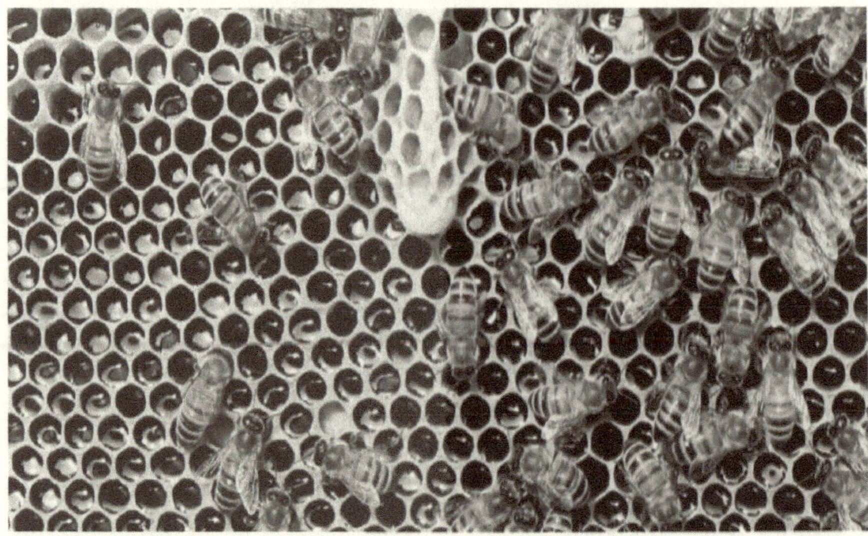

Part of examining the casings is searching for brood—covered and uncapped hatchlings and eggs. Appeared here is a lovely example of creating, uncapped hatchlings—this is the thing that you're searching for in your colony of bees review.

Search for Eggs

Distinguishing eggs is the main piece of the bee colony investigation for the new beekeeper, however, novices regularly discover the eggs hard to spot. Eggs look like meager grains of rice. There ought to be one for each cell, laid in the middle. On the off chance that you have more than one egg for each cell, your hive has laying working drones—counsels an accomplished beekeeper about the present circumstance.

The most ideal approach to see eggs is to hold the casing shifted up toward the sky at around a 30-degree point, with the brilliant sun sparkling behind you. Hold it marginally to the side of you with the goal that the shadow example of a cross-section from your shroud doesn't darken the eggs.

Utilizing understanding glasses or an amplifying glass can likewise help. You can shift the edge to and fro and try different things with the point of the sun and the edge until you see them. The base focus of the edge is generally the best spot to emphatically distinguish eggs.

Supplant the Frames

As you assess each casing, put it out from the dark space left by the past outline you eliminated. Push each edge facing the one before it as you supplant it—delicately, to try not to harm any honey bees. Utilizing a honey bee brush or smoke helps move the honey bees far removed, particularly at the edge ears, where they are probably going to get squeezed.

Assess the casings altogether, and don't change their request during an investigation. At the point when you get to the last edge, push the entire arrangement of edges together as one single unit, utilizing your hive apparatus to make space in the front for the main casing. As you supplant the primary casing, utilize your hive device to even up space on one or the other side of the first and last edges so the arrangement of edges is focused in the crate.

Supplant the Second Deep and Honey Super

With the main profound box investigated, continue to the subsequent profound box, examining the edges, and afterward restacking the crate onto the primary profound box. Supplant the sovereign excluder, if your hive has one, supplant the nectar super. To do this, position the case with the edge on the back edge of the hive, at that point gradually "destroy" it forward, moving gradually to try not to harm any honey bees. You can utilize the smoker or honey bee brush to delicately move the honey bees far removed.

Supplant the Inner Cover

Slide on the inward cover utilizing the tractor strategy: Start toward one side and gradually slide the cover across the container. Utilize the smoker or honey bee brush to move honey bees far removed, depending on the situation.

How to Uncap the Honey

The primary significant advance is to eliminate the wax covering from the brush. In business tasks, this might be finished with a programmed "uncapper" that can eliminate covers from more than 600 edges each hour. The innovation utilized in uncapping fluctuates broadly, from the programmed to the electric hand-held uncapper, and afterward to a plain blade utilized physically. This last choice includes additional time and exertion.

Despite the favored innovation, the wax covering should be taken out to get the nectar out of the brushes. Eliminating the flimsy layer of wax doesn't harm the dividers of the cells, thus the honey bees can reuse similar cells.

At times, beekeepers eliminate the nectar outlines before the honey bees cap the cells. Frequently the nectar has not yet aged, thus it has high water content. The beekeeper should then dehumidify the edges before removing the nectar.

How to Extract the Honey

Extricating the nectar implies eliminating it from the hive outlines. To do this, the uncapped edges are turned in a machine called an extractor. Radiating power draws the nectar out of the brushes and into a repository. For this cycle to function admirably, the nectar should be adequately warm to stream, as it's ideal to separate it at the earliest opportunity after the edges have been taken out from the hives, while they contain some warmth.

Something else, the casings ought to be left in a warm room preceding extricating.

Extractors change in size and in the kind of innovation they use, yet the mechanical standards contrast practically nothing. The littlest extractors are two-outline manual sorts, while some others are totally robotized, and can hold 120 edges immediately and measure more than 600 edges each hour.

How to Filter & Bottle Your Honey

After the nectar has been extricated from the casings, it goes through a progression of channels. A few tasks channel under tension, while others depend just on gravity. The interaction guarantees that no dead honey bees or different pollutions, like wax, end up in the nectar.

Contingent upon the proposed market, nectar might be packaged straightforwardly into little holders for the retail dealer or into huge drums for capacity or fare. With an end goal to speak to a wide scope of shoppers, nectar is bundled in compartments of various sizes and styles. These incorporate glass containers, plastic tubs, and squeezable containers. Like most parts of nectar preparing, packaging can include mechanization in huge tasks, or difficult work, for example, a hand valve on a plastic bucket in more modest activities.

How to aim for Honey Quality Over Quantity

Nectar evaluating in Canada started in 1935 for the fair market and in 1939 for the Canadian market. Reviewing depends on qualities, for example, dampness content, independence from unfamiliar matter, and flavor. Nectar is reviewed on a size of 1 to 3, with 1 being the best. Supermarkets for the most part sell grade 1, as lower grades are utilized in business food handling.

Nectar is likewise arranged by shading. Prepackaged nectar is delegated white, brilliant, golden, or dull. Shading is generally dictated by the sort of blossoms visited by the honey bees. All in all, light-shaded nectar is more gentle and sweet, while hazier nectar has a more grounded taste. It's about close-to-home inclination!

CHAPTER ELEVEN

HOW TO COMBINE HIVES

Some of the time in beekeeping things simply turn out poorly. Maybe there was a helpless nectar stream or a hive that just never took off because of a poor-laying sovereign. Or on the other hand, you may have a hive go queenless and choose to go along with it with another hive since you can't get another sovereign. Consolidating hives can be nerve-wracking. Luckily, there are techniques to decrease the chance of dismissal or different issues.

When to Combine Two Hives

There's no compelling reason to join hives that are working admirably all alone. However, when at least one of your hives is in a difficult situation, joining two hives may resolve the issue. Here are a few motivations to consolidate hives:

One hive is frail: Combining hives should be possible if one hive is powerless and the other is solid. If the feeble hive has a sovereign, you'll need to dispatch her before joining. You will need to keep the more grounded hive on the base and put the powerless hive on top, utilizing the solid hive's area.

One hive is queenless: If a sovereign passes on or disappears you can decide to requeen, yet some of the time a sovereign isn't accessible to buy. For this situation, consolidating the hive with another can save it. You will utilize the hive that has a sovereign as the base hive and utilize its area, putting the queenless hive on top.

Two hives are frail: Perhaps it's been a terrible year and both your hives have endured misfortunes. However long at any rate one of them has a sovereign, you can consolidate them. Or on the other hand, you can consolidate them and request another sovereign and requeen the hive. If both powerless hives have a sovereign, it's ideal to dispose of one preceding going along with them. Consolidating frail hives might be essential before winter if honey bees are light on nectar stores. Every bee colony needs in any event 70 pounds of nectar to overcome the colder time of year without starving.

The most effective method to Combine Hives

Consolidating hives is genuinely straightforward however it is ideal to be readied. Before beginning, follow these means:

Make up an answer of sugar syrup to take care of the honey bees after you consolidate the hives.

Get a sheet of paper and cut three cuts in it. The paper will permit the hives to consolidate without as much battling. The cuts permit pheromones and fragrances to be traded between the two hives. The honey bees can bite through the paper, and when they do, the honey bees will have become acclimated to one another and will be coordinated without battling.

> Light your smoker—you will need to smoke the hives well.

> Snatch a few squares of wood or concrete to put before the hive.

> When you have every one of your materials prepared, follow these means to securely and adequately consolidate two hives.

> Smoke and open the more modest hive: If the hive is in two profound boxes and can be united to one, this is the best course to follow. Take casings of honey bees, brood, and nectar and trade them for void edges in the lower profound hive body. On the off chance that both profound boxes are full or near it, leave both boxes unblemished.

> Rehash this interaction with the bigger hive: Consolidate it into one profound box if conceivable. You ought to have a limit of three profound boxes to join; more than this and there ought to be no motivation to consolidate hives.

> Set up the hives: Place the internal and external covers close to the passageway to the more grounded hive so the honey bees can discover their way into it.

> Spot the sheet of paper on top of the more grounded hive: If it's breezy, you should tape the sides to the outside of the crate so it doesn't brush off.

- ➤   Spot the case into the new hive: Move the more vulnerable hive's crate to the new hive, setting it on top of the more grounded hive delicately. Make sure to smoke everybody intensely so they are somewhat more settled during this distressing progress.

- ➤   Psyche the additional edges: If there are any additional edges or boxes that simply have a couple of honey bees (no brood or nectar) in them, place them on the squares before the new hive so the honey bees can stroll into it.

- ➤   Conceal the highest point of the consolidated hive.

- ➤   Spot the feeder on top of the consolidated hive.

Let everything be for about seven days: After seven days, check the hive to ensure the paper has been bitten through and that the hives have effectively consolidated. Ensure there are eggs.

CHAPTER TWELVE

PROTECT BEES AND BEEHIVES FROM BEARS

On the off chance that you live anyplace where bears may come to visit your colony of bees, you need to secure your honey bee yard since it won't be long before a bear pays your hives an evening time visit, leaving harm and obliteration afterward. Bears are exceptionally pulled in to nectar and honey bee brood, and may choose to visit a hive unexpectedly if they are not satisfied with food around them during summer seasons. Spring—when hungry bears alert from their colder time of year hibernation—and fall, when bears are building fat stores in anticipation of winter, are the most probable occasions for a bear to visit your hives, however, your honey bee yard is weak practically any season.

How to Protect and Prevent Beehive From Bears

Secure and Prevent

If a bear visits your hive, the harm may be insignificant, just dispersed boxes, a couple of paw swipes across outlines. Or on the other hand, it very well may be broader, with hive boxes annihilated and outlines tore separated or in any event, missing! What's more awful, when a bear builds up a desire for honey bees and honey bee brood, he will be back for more—in any event, visiting a similar hive a few evenings in succession.

So what's a beekeeper to do? Perhaps the best approach to keep mountain bears from harming your colonies of bees is to set up electric net fencing. The electric wall can be accused of batteries, sun-oriented, or power straightforwardly. You should hold vegetation under the fence clear, or, more than likely the charge won't be adequately critical. Also, you would prefer not to hold back the vacillating charger since it takes a decent shock of flow to get past the thick layer of hiding and fat on a bear. Also, as I took in the most difficult way possible, an electric wall should be connected to be viable! Bears can tell from some distance if a fence is charged, and they will walk directly through it if it's not charged. Truth be told, a few beekeepers prescribe goading the fence with bacon to get the bear to stop adequately long to realize what an electrified barrier is. Something else, the bear may walk directly through the fence without getting stunned long enough to take note.

Beehive Proper Placement

The situation of your bee colonies can likewise help keep bears and different hunters from visiting. Although you need a hive in dappled daylight, try not to put hives close to the forested areas. At any rate, 300 feet from the woods' edge is a decent rule. Keeping grasses cut for a distance around the hives can help also. A bear doesn't care to be out in the open without cover. This additionally puts blossoming plants at a further separation from your honey bees.

Beehive Fencing

Rather than electric net fencing, you can utilize numerous strands of electric wire or woven wire connected to wood, steel, or fiberglass posts. Utilize an electric or sun-oriented charger, an energizer, and a battery to control these walls too. Poly tape and wire are different choices for the electric wall to keep out bears.

Ensure that whatever electrified barrier framework you use, your fence is in any event 3 1/2 feet high, with wire strands close to 8 inches separated on a perpetual fence, and 12 inches separated on a brief fence. The base wire should be close to 8 crawls off the ground. Ensure that your energizer gives at any rate 4-5,000 volts of stun—yet on the off chance that you utilize this, be cautious as it tends to be a peril to people too. Utilize a decent ground pole, and add a tangle of chicken wire or metal material around the border of the fence, on the ground, to guarantee the bear is grounded when contacts the fence.

At last, ensure that your colonies of bees are in any event 3 feet from your fence, in any case, a bear can reach through the fence and swipe at the hives without really going through it.

On the off chance that you do endure bear-related bee colony harm, check with your nearby helpful augmentation office—you might be qualified for some financial remuneration to supplant your harmed hardware and honey bees. Additionally, in certain regions, monetary help is accessible for setting up the wall to discourage bears.

CONCLUSION

Now that you realize you have the craving, you realize you have the interest, you realize you have the opportunity. So how would you begin beekeeping? These eight hints assembled from veteran beekeepers are every one of those things they wish they'd known before they got their first hive.

✓   Utilize New Equipment. Of course, utilized gear is modest or free, yet it might well additionally have issues that an amateur will not perceive or have the option to fix. Start new with new hives and new casings to save yourself a superfluous migraine.

Note: If reusing old gear is essential to you, have an accomplished beekeeper look at it for you and ensure you have a beekeeping tutor who can help you on the off chance that you experience issues.

✓   Start Early In the Season. Ask beekeeping assets in your general vicinity to figure out the opportune chance to begin a settlement. You would prefer not to begin too soon before the honey bees will want to discover food and keep warm, yet you would prefer not to begin so late that they don't have the opportunity to make sufficient nectar for the colder time of year or have missed the primary huge push of nectar.

✓   Keep It Simple. At the point when you start, simply center on learning fundamental honey beekeeping strategies. Hold experimentation to the base. Gain proficiency with the proven first until you have set up, sound hives.

✓   Check Your "Should Have" List Twice. Before you request anything, ensure you understand what the piece of gear is for and why you need it. Everybody winds up beekeeping in their particular manner and has their peculiarities and inclinations. Hold your underlying buys to the things you need to begin: hives, honey bees, a smoker, and defensive stuff.

✓   Start With Italian Bees. Italian honey bees are the norm in the U.S. They are usually accessible, known to experienced beekeepers you may go to for help, and are not difficult to deal with.

✓   Start With a Nucleus Colony. Beginning with a core province, or "bundle," of honey bees will allow you to set up a state, which will train you a ton about honey bees and bringing honey bees up in your particular conditions. Gathering wild multitudes is famous in numerous beekeeping gatherings, yet they aren't the most ideal alternative for amateur beekeepers.

✓   Think about Having Two Colonies. This may appear to be nonsensical since two provinces are more work than one. Two states will give both of you things: the opportunity to analyze settlements, which will help you spot issues prior because you'll see a distinction, and a province to work within the event that you lose one, which is normal with fledgling beekeepers.

✓   Know You May Not Have Honey That First Year. Contingent upon your area and the climate that year, it isn't exceptional that the new state of honey bees wouldn't deliver sufficient overflow nectar their first year for you to collect any. Beekeeping is something to take up with a long view. There is, from multiple points of view, no closure game in beekeeping.